Out-worn heart,
in a time out-worn,
Come clear of the nets of
wrong and right;
Laugh, heart, again in
the grey twilight.

—*William Butler Yeats*

CONTENTS

Introduction	6
Major Arcana	7
Minor Arcana	52
Readings	113
Author's Note	125

INTRODUCTION

Welcome to the *Nightfall Tarot*, a darkened interpretation of the classic Rider-Waite-Smith Tarot. Whether you're new to the world of Tarot or a longtime practitioner, this deck stays true to the original meanings developed by Arthur Waite and Pamela Colman Smith, although there have been some updates to many of the symbols and scenes.

In this deck you'll find Norse runes, Icelandic staves, Wiccan designs, astrology, and other chthonic symbols alongside many of the original Judeo-Christian motifs, creating a more accessible and multicultural experience of Tarot in the 21st century. With darkness being ever present in the *Nightfall Tarot*'s illustrations, each unique card is tinged with melancholy, pulling you deeper into the shadowy areas of your life, and revealing truths in the grey twilight.

AMORY ABBOTT

Nightfall
tarot

4880 Lower Valley Road, Atglen, PA 19310

Copyright © 2023 by Amory Abbott

Library of Congress Control Number: 2022944529

All rights reserved. No part of this work may be reproduced or used in any form or by any means—graphic, electronic, or mechanical, including photocopying or information storage and retrieval systems—without written permission from the publisher.

The scanning, uploading, and distribution of this book or any part thereof via the Internet or any other means without the permission of the publisher is illegal and punishable by law. Please purchase only authorized editions and do not participate in or encourage the electronic piracy of copyrighted materials.

"Red Feather Mind Body Spirit" logo is a trademark of Schiffer Publishing, Ltd.
"Red Feather Mind Body Spirit Feather" logo is a registered trademark of Schiffer Publishing, Ltd.

Designed by Danielle D. Farmer
Cover design by Danielle D. Farmer
Type set in Scotch Display/Expressway

ISBN: 978-0-7643-6623-9
Printed in China

Published by REDFeather Mind, Body, Spirit
An imprint of Schiffer Publishing, Ltd.
4880 Lower Valley Road
Atglen, PA 19310
Phone: (610) 593-1777; Fax: (610) 593-2002
Email: Info@redfeathermbs.com
Web: www.redfeathermbs.com

REDFeather Mind, Body, Spirit's titles are available at special discounts for bulk purchases for sales promotions or premiums. Special editions, including personalized covers, corporate imprints, and excerpts, can be created in large quantities for special needs. For more information, contact the publisher.

MAJOR ARCANA

0—The Fool

*New beginnings, youth,
carefree, recklessness*

The Fool's journey begins with a naive start, unaware of the joys and sorrows ahead. They walk in a daydream, richly dressed, an inadequate bag over their shoulder, a scented rose, and a dog as a companion. It's all very novel, but will they see the cliff ahead? Whether they fall or catch themselves, real experience is soon on its way.

Reversed
Caution, anxiety, lack of spontaneity

I—The Magician

*Creativity, confidence,
the ability to create change*

The Magician stands with a scepter raised to the sky and a finger pointing to the earth. In between, all things are possible. The four elemental objects of the Tarot—wand, cup, sword, pentacle—rest on the table, symbolizing that all of his power is available to him at this moment, and it is time to act.

Reversed
Abuse of power, lack of pure intention,
or self-doubt

II—The High Priestess

*Intuition, wisdom,
stillness in mind and action*

The High Priestess embodies pure feminine energy, peace, and personal depth. She sits at the gate of a temple with light and dark columns, the moon at her feet and its phases in her crown, a calm ocean behind her ornate curtain. She rests, deep in reflection, seeking wisdom from inside herself.

Reversed
A need to communicate internal thoughts clearly to others, to vocalize feelings

III—The Empress

Passion, connection to the natural world, motherhood

The Empress relaxes on a pile of ornate cushions in a lush forest. Pregnant, and surrounded by feminine symbols, a crown of twelve stars on her head, she openly basks in her sexuality and power, passion flowing like the waterfall behind her.

Reversed
Intellect blocking the sensual, an inability or trouble creating new things

IV—The Emperor

Authority, creating structure, fatherhood

The Emperor sits sternly on his horned throne, with towering and barren mountains behind him. Clad both in protective armor and lavish robes, he holds a staff topped with an ankh—the Egyptian symbol of life—reluctant, perhaps, to take up the harsh responsibility of authority and rule, for the prosperity of society.

Reversed
Immaturity or irresponsible use of power, or an overabundance of gentleness

V—The Hierophant

Tradition, conformity, spiritual principles

The Hierophant stands at a pulpit, fingers raised to heaven, and crossed fingers pointing below. Standing strong in their principles, the opulent Hierophant interprets and disseminates the laws of his beliefs and commits to them, trusting in the mystery and guidance of the divine.

Reversed
Rebelliousness or nonconformity, rejection of the status quo

VI—The Lovers

Love, harmony, chosen partnership

Two lovers stand before a divine spirit crowned in shimmering leaves. It offers them the gifts of knowledge (the apple) and power (the spark), joining their minds and hearts in unity. Before them a vast mountain rises, a testament to what can be accomplished in a strong partnership.

Reversed
A unity that was not chosen or is no longer harmonious

VII—The Chariot

Willpower, directed energy, achievement

Under a starred canopy, the rider stands confident in her chariot, the Magician's scepter in hand, the High Priestess's moon-shaped armor on her shoulders, smiling as she departs from the walled castle city. The two sphinxes, free of controlling reigns, seem to be guided by the rider's will alone. The rider is embarking on an epic journey of her own making.

Reversed
Setbacks, roadblocks, or difficulty finding a passionate direction

VIII—Strength

Belief in yourself, fortitude, inner power

A woman in ceremonial robes stands barefoot in a field, holding a bouquet of wildflowers. She has tamed a lion, but not by means of physical might or threatening appearance. The infinity symbol above her head shows that her strength within never falters. True strength—the strength that tames the lion of the self—comes from an inner confidence, through grace, patience, and gentleness.

Reversed
Emotional weakness, self-doubt,
or destructive tendencies

IX—The Hermit

Solitude, discovering inner truths, wisdom

A cloaked figure wanders the mountains, seeking time alone, but not lonely. To be a Hermit is to isolate yourself from influences from the outside world to better understand your own internal world. This card also suggests that in lonely dark places, the brightness of the inner self can light the way like a lantern.

Reversed
Alternatively, a need to seek out community for wisdom, or a fear of being alone

X—Wheel of Fortune

Luck, destiny, karma

This Wheel of Fortune features a Veqvisir, an Icelandic stave symbol used to guide travelers through rough weather. It is encircled by the Ouroboros—a serpent eating its own tail—to symbolize the cycle of death and rebirth. Surrounding the wheel in a storm are the four natural elements wind, water, fire, and earth, guiding each safely toward their destiny, in the endless cycle of self-renewal.

Reversed
Feeling out of control, or addicted to chance

XI – Justice

Honesty, truth, authenticity

The Justice figure strides boldly with a balanced scale held aloft, eyes facing forward insistently, a sword at the ready behind her to strike down falsehood. This card arrives at a moment in life when self-truths must come to light, be faced head on, and find reconciliation.

Reversed
Stuck in an unfair situation, or unable to face a hard reality

XII – The Hanged Man

Self-sacrifice, dedication, uniqueness

The man hangs of his own free will, arms reaching out openly, an almost ecstatic look on his face. His tunic is emblazoned with the Norse rune associated with Tyr, a mythic hero who sacrificed his own hand to keep the ferocious wolf Fenrir captive. The Hanged Man finds themselves dedicated to an idea or belief or inner truth, giving themselves to it wholeheartedly.

Reversed

Feeling taken advantage of, giving into social pressures or labels

XIII—Death

Endings, transition, inevitable change

Death rides clad in dark armor, at the edge of the sea. It has delivered kings and priests to the funeral ship beyond yet now lays down its Lutheran banner in the presence of a child approaching unafraid, holding a bouquet of fresh flowers. The Death card is not a portent of death, but rather the recognition that an important transition is on its way that must be embraced without fear.

Reversed
Stagnation, fear of change, feeling unprepared for something new

XIV – Temperance

Patience, tolerance, finding balance

To be tempered is to become stronger through experience. In this card, an angel stands with one foot on land, connected to the earth, and one foot in a shimmering pool, stepping into the nonphysical realm. They pour a liquid magically between two cups, biding their time, as spring flowers bloom. A path—symbolic of a life's journey—leads from the pool far beyond to a mountain peak topped in a crown of light.

Reversed
Loss of control, restless or extreme behavior

XV—The Devil

Addictive behavior, seduction, illusion

A fiendish couple stands chained to an altar, their tails bearing fruit (life) and fire (destruction), and they have summoned the Devil. The towering beast points two fingers toward heaven and a blazing torch toward the underworld, signifying that between the two, good or bad habits, relationships, or activities, it is all a matter of what one chooses to chain themselves to.

Reversed
Acting responsibly, seeing through illusions, liberation

XVI—The Tower

Cataclysm, upheaval, release

An unpredictable blast of lightning has struck the Tower, throwing the king and queen from the height of their lives, fire engulfing their home and cherished possessions. The king is decrowned, separated from his partner, and in free fall. The stone monolith they have worked so hard to build is crumbling before their eyes as they plummet toward uncertainty. Dramatic change has been thrust upon them, suddenly, and their only choice is to ride out the storm.

Reversed
Crisis without change, a lack of closure or recourse

XVII—The Star

Recovery, optimism, finding peace

Like the Temperance card, we find a figure approaching a pool; however, under a bright guiding Star, this figure is nude, stripped of all defenses, left humbled and exposed in her true form. She calmly pours shining water from two bowls in an offering of self, stepping across the surface of the water—which represents the subconscious realm—in full awareness.

Reversed
Hopelessness, doubt, or an inability to be completely honest

XVIII—The Moon

Ancient wisdom, wild instinct, deep mystery

The Moon rises in its full form on a dark night, reflected in the murky water below. Holding sway over the wild things of the world, its eternal cycle is a reminder of our connection to the deepest parts of our psychic selves, that invisible forces tug at the essence of our being and drive us toward deeper knowing, intuition, and, occasionally, madness.

Reversed
Emotional turmoil, depression, or stuck in surface feelings

XIX—The Sun

Joy, clarity, liberation

There is undeniable radiance and wholeness in the bright light of the Sun. The world is clear, the ground is nourished, warmth permeates the air, the birds and flowers rejoice. Mystery, shadows, and truth are brought into the light and set free. Simple pleasures, good health, and emotional ease are in full bloom.

Reversed
Happiness touched with sorrow, melancholy, nostalgic for joys of the past

XX—Judgment

Rejuvenation, reckoning, good things coming to fruition

An angel's trumpet sounds, calling lost souls to rise and rejoice. A great decision has been made; a great moment of awakening has arrived. The world is being made right, and the time of prosperity is here. The soul celebrates when it is recognized and renewed.

Reversed
A lack of faith or trust, fear or unacceptance of change

XXI—The World

Completion, wholeness, great wisdom

A cosmic figure dances with two wands, ushering in the culmination of all things. The planet eclipses the sun, and we see the World in our greatest moment. The satisfaction of a job well done, the rest at a long journey's end, the wisdom achieved from a powerful experience, healing and gratitude for difficult events from the past.

Reversed
Delays, but not failure;
more unexpected work to be done

MINOR ARCANA

Wands

Ace of Wands
New beginnings, life force, adventure

In a dark and quiet place, a hand emerges from the clouds to present new life. This is the gift of Wands—action, masculine energy, enthusiasm, and the element of fire—a boost of energy to make new things happen, and the impulse to act when needed.

Reversed
Hesitation, laziness, or a false start

Two of Wands
A choice between security and adventure, risk

A woman stands on the threshold of a fortress, the wide world beyond. One wand stands ungrowing and anchored to the solid stone foundation behind her, the other wand with new leaves, in her hand as a walking stick. The world rests safely in her other hand, but nevertheless she must choose between two lives.

Reversed
A choice has already been made, but with unexpected or unwanted results

Three of Wands
A call beyond the familiar, longing

From a high plateau, a man gazes wistfully out to sea. Two wands have taken root in the rock behind him, yet the one in his hand still wants to move, to travel. No matter what foundations have been set in life, the mind still dreams of journeys untaken and ideas not explored. The sea is calling.

Reversed
Nesting, taking root somewhere, a loss of independence

Four of Wands
Structure, recovery, a return to convention

Two friends meet on a long bridge. Perhaps one is returning home from a long time away, or the two have cause for celebration. Four wands frame their reunion, and beyond, a castle and mountain; symbols of structure, propriety, and strength, and the joy of homecoming.

Reversed
According to Arthur Waite, the meaning remains the same: an emphasis on structure and security

Five of Wands
*Good-natured competition,
but unclear direction*

A group of men challenge each other with crossed wands. Are they fighting? Building something? Perhaps they are practicing a performance? Whatever the interpretation, there is disorder, and a lack of clear purpose. Their individual movements are making collaboration difficult, and clarity won't be reached until they can work together.

Reversed
Sabotage, rancor, an inability to negotiate needs

Six of Wands
Leadership, confidence, success at a surface level

A man rides atop a decorated horse, parading before a group of soldiers. With a wreath of victory tied to his wand, is he delivering an inspiring speech? The man's high status is clear, but his popularity is questionable, as seen on the faces of his followers. Sometimes success is achieved merely through one's own confidence, and not always by popularity.

Reversed
Having an unpopular opinion, or a pessimistic outlook

Seven of Wands
Caught off-guard, going on the defensive

A man has been ambushed, forced up a hill to defend against the threats below. His mismatched shoes, bitter expression, and fighting stance suggest the attack was unexpected, possibly a betrayal or mutiny, and that a multitude of problems must be faced without time for preparation.

Reversed
Feeling boxed in, taken hostage, or a lack of organization

Eight of Wands
Healthy momentum, an organized and unified front

Like a volley of arrows, eight wands sail in formation toward the earth on a stormy night. Amid the chaos and rain, all the wands' energy is harmonious, allied toward a common target. This card finds a collective effort aimed at one goal, and flying true.

Reversed
Inability to stay focused, or one considerable threat from the outside

Nine of Wands
Courage, persistence, resourcefulness

Beaten and bruised, a young man stands defending himself from within a cage of wands. See how the man has uprooted a wand and created a path out of what has ensnared him? The things that formed a cage around him may be the very things that provide a means of escape.

Reversed
Playing the victim, cowardice, Stockholm syndrome

Ten of Wands
Overcommitment, too many burdens, stubbornness

A woman carries ten wands haphazardly toward a house far in the distance. The loose bundle forces her into an awkward posture, blocking her face from the path ahead. Without the ability to see where her next step will fall, her burden of ten wands has unnecessarily made the journey more treacherous, frustrating, and time consuming.

Reversed
Using caution, asking for help, or shared responsibility

Page of Wands
Young energy, enthusiasm for new beginnings

A young woman in fine robes stands at the ready, holding a wand with new leaves budding. Her lower coat has a pattern of fiery salamanders—creatures of intense energy—her expression is one of excitement and intrigue. New adventures lie ahead, as mysterious as the distant pyramids.

Reversed
Cautious to a fault, hesitant to take chances

Knight of Wands
Courage, boldness, the thrill of adventure

A knight rears into action atop his horse, a fiery salamander as his sigil of untamed energy. Across from the same pyramids as the Page of Wands, the knight thrives in this place of mystery and intrigue. This card comes to those at a time of daring acts, and strong will.

Reversed
Overconfident and unprepared, biting off more than one can chew

Queen of Wands
Self-confidence, generosity, fierce passion

A youthful queen sits in her lion throne holding a budding wand, and a sunflower in full bloom. With a docile cat as a companion, she is open to life; arms wide, passionate, alluring, and thriving even in the harshest environment.

Reversed
Impatient with those who don't know what they want, or stifled desire

King of Wands
Forthright manners, confident and direct leadership

Layered in armor and opulent robes and furs, a king sits on a decorated throne, his gaze turned far away to other thoughts and dreams. He rules with curtness, impatient with anyone who takes too much of his time or distracts him from daydream. A fiery salamander approaches his feet, inviting him to adventures he knows he cannot leave his throne to experience.

Reversed
Resenting responsibilities, listlessness, or lazy leadership

Cups

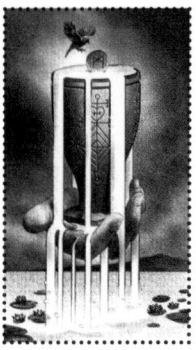

Ace of Cups
The many forms of love, emotional and spiritual nourishment

A cup carved with an Icelandic love charm overflows like a fountain. A coin bearing the Norse rune symbolizing *self* drops into the cup as an offering. This is the gift of Cups—love, feminine energy, healing, awareness—an overflowing of the purest divine grace, presented as an unconditional gift.

Reversed
Feelings of emptiness, or an inability to recognize love

Two of Cups
*Connection, commitment,
a meaningful relationship*

A young couple offers each other cups of warm liquid in a private ceremony, the steam rising between them as their energies intertwine. Having committed to each other in this serious and solemn way, their future calls to them in a secluded home built from their meaningful bond.

Reversed
Friendship over romance, or a loss of intimacy

Three of Cups
Community, deep bonds, celebration

Three close friends dance and toast in a field full of bountiful harvest. A recognition is needed in the reward of laborious work, the nourishment of close friendships, or the accomplishments of a dedicated group. It is a time to honor the efforts of collective action.

Reversed
Unfinished business, or work putting strain on a friendship

Four of Cups
Hesitation, indifference, unseen opportunities

A cup appears as an unexpected gift to a young woman reclining under a tree. She appears dissatisfied with the three familiar cups that sit before her in the grass, but is reluctant to acknowledge or perhaps simply fails to notice the wavering gift of more insight, love, or emotional depth that the fourth cup has to offer.

Reversed
Hindsight about a previous opportunity, or the consequences of rejecting a gift

Five of Cups
Hindsight, grief, a failure to recognize what remains

A woman stands on the opposite bank of a homestead, having spilled three cups on the ground. Is she a widow? What has she lost from those cups? Does she not see that there are still two cups upright on the blanket behind her? Perhaps the blanket is a memory of when two cups was enough.

Reversed
A lingering joy that goes unseen or is shrouded by an overpowering sorrow

Six of Cups
Being taken care of, nostalgia, learning from others

A young woman and a small boy stand at a well, the woman showing the boy how to arrange flowers in their cups. Their house is modest, they have few possessions, but there is an act of learning and love taking place, possibly in the form of a memory of the past, from childhood. It is a time of acknowledging what has been learned from an elder.

Reversed
Disconnected from or unable to reconcile the past

Seven of Cups
Imagination, wonder, great opportunities

Seven cups magically appear before an astonished figure, each symbolizing something desirable: inheritance, fame, security, material goods, physical pleasure, food, valor. A myriad of goals can be envisioned, but a choice must be made to see them become reality.

Reversed
Fantasies not grounded in possibility, unrealistic desires

Eight of Cups
Accepting change, a higher calling, moving on

By a quiet shoreline, a table is set with eight cups, but one place remains empty. An aging figure makes their way slowly away from the table, setting out on a journey. Perhaps it is to find the ninth and final cup, or perhaps it is simply moving on to other things. Either way, the time has come to strike out again, to seek the next thing, to begin the next stage of life.

Reversed
Not a time to forfeit or leave something behind, but to stay and give it greater attention

Nine of Cups
Material success, smugness, self-satisfaction

A man sits proud in front of a table of cups, surrounding him like an audience, like trophies, like milestones of his life. He is satisfied with his accomplishments, although perhaps only at a surface level. Nevertheless, it is a moment of pleasure, a moment to gloat, a moment to be proud of what success has come.

Reversed
Personal sacrifices for the needs of others, or generosity getting in the way of prosperity

Ten of Cups
Fulfilled promises, blessings, culmination

A family rejoices under a rainbow of shining cups. They wonder at the fruits of their labor and bask in the reality of the life they created together. There is an abundance of joy, a cause for celebration, a dream that has come to fruition at last.

Reversed
Hunger not satiated, or not appreciating what has been achieved

Page of Cups
Wonder, fascination, deep curiosity

A young person clad in a lotus-patterned tunic stands at the edge of the ocean, raising a cup before them. A fish emerges from the cup and speaks with the page, perhaps telling them the secrets and wonders of the ocean beyond. The page stands transfixed in awe of the fish, and what magic exists in the underwater realm.

Reversed
Logic subduing the imagination, or a fear of the subconscious

Knight of Cups
Enchantment, obsession, a love of fantasy

A knight rides quietly on her horse, carefully holding a cup in front of her. The fish on her cloak appear rising to the surface of the water, her helm a delicate pair of wings, as if she has found a way to fly away from the depths of the sea. She moves slowly toward adventure, transfixed on the cup like some holy grail, perhaps lost in a daydream.

Reverse
Unable to escape the demands of reality, boredom

Queen of Cups
Creative and selfless love, dedication to one's self and the world

The Queen of Cups holds a large, decorated cup, perhaps an urn, up to the ocean in a private ceremony. Her robes drape over her knees, one shifting from fabric to water, as she begins to blend with the sea. In this, she offers her entire being—emotions, actions, attention, and intelligence—to the world before her, in a blessing of love.

Reversed
Acting disingenuous, or lost in one's internal world

King of Cups
Creativity channeled into work, manifesting fantasy in the real world

A king sits on his throne, adrift at sea. With a loose grip on his lotus scepter, he looks beyond, eyes locked on something or someone, raising his cup to them. In the distance, a ship finds shore with the help of a lighthouse. This king has found a way to rule with imagination and compassion.

Reversed
Blocked creativity, or a lack of honesty about true feelings

Swords

Ace of Swords
Singleness of mind, spiritual truth at all costs

Above lofty mountain peaks, a sword is thrust into the sky. The dual edges cut through the air with clarity and razor-sharp purpose, and through this act, rewards come effortlessly: a crown, honor, and prosperity. This is the gift of Swords—mental acuity, morality, and the element of air—an unobstructed view of the workings of all things, and the ability to process them.

Reversed
Confusion, a lack of clarity, or one who is using their mind to manipulate others

Two of Swords
Closed-off emotions, a bittersweet choice

A young woman sits blindfolded before a small inlet, hair grown long, guarding herself, and perhaps the ocean itself (the spiritual realm), from anyone that comes too close. Her stoicism is a strength but comes at a difficult cost. She is able to defend herself confidently, yet she is blindfolded, unable to recognize friend from foe, blessing from threat.

Reversed
Emotional vulnerability, or a lack of healthful boundaries

Three of Swords
Heartbreak, love lost, deep sorrow

A heart with the rune of "love" has turned to stone, pierced by three swords amid a rainstorm. The message of this card is clear—pain, loss, despair—yet the heart turns cold and hard in the wake of an unbearable hurt only in order to protect itself. It knows what it must do in order to heal.

Reversed
Letting go, recovery, or avoiding the steps one must take to grieve a loss

Four of Swords
Reprieve, healthful withdrawal, internal healing

A knight rests atop an open tomb, surrounded by the swords of a great battle. Is the knight flesh and blood, or merely a stone sculpture? Either way, a deep rest is being taken, inner peace being sought; recovery is being made from trauma.

Reversed
An inability to turn the attention inward, no rest from trauma

Five of Swords
Embarrassment, defeat, a sullied reputation

Twin brothers have fought along the sandy shore. The solemn victor walks away bruised; the defeated twin weeps on his knees, critically wounded. The battle was not won by either, but rather an unnecessary dispute has escalated and left both ashamed, and in bitter regret.

Reversed
A last chance to reconcile before harm is done, a humble perspective

Six of Swords
Emotional burdens, keeping secrets, the weight of knowledge

A weeping woman holds her child as they are ferried across a body of water to foggy cliffs in the distance. This image resembles Charon, the boatman who carries the dead across the River Styx to the afterlife, but with the addition of six swords as cargo. Many will take secrets to the grave, as truth dies with them, a bitter and heavy weight to bear.

Reversed
Breaking tradition, exposing long-hidden truths, letting go

Seven of Swords
Impulsive action, cleverness, opportunistic deception

A thief sneaks away under a full moon with five swords stolen from a group of men huddled at a campfire. Opportunities have been seized through devious action, a betrayal perhaps, or an enemy's defenses weakened through cleverness. Two swords remain, however, symbolizing that a problem may have been lessened but not solved for good.

Reversed
Resisting temptation, seeking the help of others, or getting to the heart of the matter

Eight of Swords
Gaslighting, feeling helpless, oppression

A woman crouches at the shore, blindfolded and wrapped in ribbons as the tide comes in. A wall of swords line her sides, an illusion of entrapment, as a shadowy figure watches from a distant hilltop. Without her sight, the woman cannot see that her bonds are loose, the swords are not a cage, and that she may break free at any time. To escape, she must sense beyond what can be seen, and trust her intuition.

Reversed
Coming to one's senses, discovering inner strength, or seeking help

Nine of Swords
Haunting thoughts, anxiety, obsession

A person sits up in bed, tormented by their thoughts, ghostly swords flying in and out of their mind. They lie under a blanket decorated in zodiac symbols—all of the ways life expresses itself in us—and perhaps it is comforting or perhaps it is overwhelming, but nevertheless, a myriad of thoughts keeps them restless and in anguish.

Reversed
Facing a difficult truth, interference from the outside

Ten of Swords
Excessive emotional turmoil, taking on too many responsibilities

A figure lies dead, draped in a shining cloak, ten swords run through them. While one sword is deadly enough, this card represents the epitome of excessive thoughts and actions. Like an overload of stress, or working oneself to death, unsustainable momentum leads to exhaustion and complete failure. Nevertheless, the sun rises slowly in the distance, and hope lives on.

Reversed
Pain averted temporarily, or the release from overwhelming burdens

Page of Swords
Skepticism, concern for what may happen

We see a young man standing larger than life, sword resting uneasily, ready to take action. His expression suggests that he has a reason for distrust and wariness, but also a determination to do what must be done.

Reversed
Overly trusting, or prone to gullibility

Knight of Swords
Swift action, courage, hasty decisions

A knight charges headlong into battle, his shield and tack feature butterflies, his chest plate an eagle, swift and bold creatures who throw caution to the wind. Even with the sun rising in his eyes, he rides fiercely into the fray. Some may find him reckless or foolhardy, but nevertheless his courage is hard to match.

Reversed
Aggression without virtue, not fighting for a good cause, only for pleasure

Queen of Swords
Wisdom, resilience, grace born from sorrow

A queen holds her sword up with conviction, a hand outstretched in a gentle offering, or perhaps reaching for the memory of something lost. All around her are symbols of metamorphosis and resilience in the form of butterflies on her crown and throne. Many see this queen as a widow; someone who has faced death or loss and transformed into something more beautiful.

Reversed
Corrupted or consumed by grief, or a hiatus from responsibilities

King of Swords
Thriving when put in command, working for the common good

A stern king sits uneasy in his obelisk throne, looking ready to stand and act. Sword at the ready, hand braced, his gaze is sharp and piercing, his mind swift and calculating. Snow piles around the throne, the wind pulling at the ribbons of his cape. He is ready to fight for truth and take control.

Reversed
Prolonging important decisions, or serving the self instead of others

Pentacles

Ace of Pentacles
Sure footing, a sanctuary to safely grow from

A hand reaches through the trees over a lakeside cabin, bearing the gift of Pentacles—nature, physical health, security, the element of earth—to prosper in the physical world. Whether an inheritance, a place of reprieve, or a healthful lifestyle, this card offers a head start in physical and spiritual wealth.

Reversed
Loss of material security, or forced from a comfortable situation

Two of Pentacles
Finding balance between responsibilities, juggling contradictory needs

On a stage set in a turbulent sea, a man dances with two pentacle discs, his arms linked in an infinite loop. Two seemingly separate choices are revealed to be dependent on each other, providing balance and counterweight, lest the whole act fall apart. It appears to be a comical routine, making light of some deeper struggle, just like the prop boats riding high on the waves behind him.

Reversed
An imbalance of work and life, or burning the candle at both ends

Three of Pentacles
Expertise, collaboration, cooperation

A stone mason, an architect, and a priest look over their plans for a cathedral. Each one brings a special understanding and skill to its construction, design, and purpose, and together they are creating something magnificent. To work at the highest level will attract others, and lead to greater endeavors that could not be accomplished alone.

Reversed
Skills that are held back or unappreciated, or mediocrity that requires more experience

Four of Pentacles
Material status, miserly behavior, arrogance

A man sits in a throne in a town square, flaunting his wealth with the pentacle discs he owns. His mind is set on material possessions, as symbolized by his pentacle crown, but the large disc at his feet suggests he is unknowingly weighed down and trapped by his own greed. Leaving his stationary throne is a risk that requires him to lift the disc from his feet, multiplied in turn that he must first set down the discs in his hands to do so.

Reversed
Finite resources, selflessness, or a lack of structure

Five of Pentacles
Victimhood, feeling outcast, inequity

Two people walk the snowy streets at night, underdressed for the cold, clothes tattered, bandaged limbs, and needing crutches. A bell swings from the man's neck, warning society of his disease. A summer scene is illuminated through the windows of a church, but they have no way inside. They are unwelcome, but they are not alone, having found solidarity through adversity.

Reversed
Charity, recovery, support from society or a cultural sea change

Six of Pentacles
Generosity, equity, goodwill

A matriarch gives thanks to the land and trees around her, and the bounty of pentacle discs on the table before her. Her appreciation is shared by two men who have come to combine the wealth of their respective nations, so that they all may prosper. Gratitude and unity will ensure the health of everyone.

Reversed
Denial or fear of asking for help, or selfishness

Seven of Pentacles
Smart planning, labor, and reward

A man has arrived at a garden looking weary, but ready to work. Is he there to harvest his bounty, or is he there because more work needs to be done? Either way, careful planning has been needed, and may still. Good work yields good results.

Reversed
Unexpected tasks, more work despite what has been completed

Eight of Pentacles
Dedication, consistency, steady progress

A master carver sits at her bench carving pentacle discs, one by one. Each is unique, made with focus and care, each more skillfully carved than the last. When one enjoys what they do, it ceases to feel like "work," and the more one practices, the more valuable their skill becomes.

Reversed
Lack of passion or long-term goals, or alternatively advancement to other work

Nine of Pentacles
Making something of one's life, the fruits of one's labor

A woman stands amid a lush hedge, nine pentacle discs nestled among the leaves. She holds a hooded falcon, ready to release it as the wind builds. The conditions are perfect, the hard work is done, wealth is all around, life is good; it is time to soar.

Reversed
Feeling unsatisfied, or having done unsatisfactory work toward a goal

Ten of Pentacles
Culmination, leaving a legacy, moving on

An old crone in a rune-clad coat walks joyously with her cat companion away from a happy family on a bridge. The family looks beyond to the tower cottage in a loving embrace. The old woman could be the grandmother, or a Yaga spirit, blessing the family with an inheritance or simply accumulated wealth. A chapter ends.

Reversed
Self-reliance, independence, or giving up security for adventure

Page of Pentacles
Dedicated study, seeding the future

A young boy marvels at a pentacle coin, as if it were the first one he'd ever held. He knows the wealth it represents—material and immaterial—and the potential of the knowledge and strengths he will gain along the way of a life well lived. Having found a special place of his own beyond the valley, he is excited to begin.

Reversed
Getting ahead of one's self, taking detracting shortcuts

Knight of Pentacles
Diligence, devotion to a task, selflessness

A knight rests in his saddle, holding a pentacle disc as one would hold an object of their own creation that took great efforts to craft. Perhaps returning home from a great battle, he sits reflecting on the hard work he's accomplished, taking one last moment to himself before crossing the fields and beginning the next adventure.

Reversed
Struggling to slow one's momentum after a task is complete, or distraction from duty

Queen of Pentacles
Immersed in the physical world, deep presence, security in life

A queen rests in a throne piled high with cushions and cloth, along a path at the edge of a forest. Having removed herself from the town in the distance, she takes time to appreciate the pentacle disc in her hand and tends to the wildlife that comes to visit her. She is deeply in tune with the natural world, happy, fulfilled, and right where she wants to be.

Reversed
Closed off from the natural world, stuck in crisis management

King of Pentacles
Social grace, pride in one's success, generosity toward others

A king sits on his ox-head throne among a lush garden of grapevines, flowering hedges, cedar saplings, and squash. These are the fruits of many labors, all growing inside the walls of a large kingdom. The king appears quite pleased with himself; not in arrogance, but genuine satisfaction with the wealth and prosperity he has created for himself and his people.

Reversed
A loss of physical security, or feeling that what one has is not enough

Readings are the way practitioners search through the darkness and mystery to bring each participant's story to light. Be it a single card, or a multitude of cards, each "spread" provides a different breadth and depth of engagement to the experience. Following is a selection of three common spreads that are ubiquitous in modern Tarot. If you are new to Tarot, these spreads are listed in order of complexity. It's suggested that you try the first before moving on. If you are a seasoned Tarot practitioner, these will, I hope, be a refreshing interpretation of the classics.

READINGS

ONE-CARD DRAW

FOR THE QUESTION AT HAND.

This is the simplest and most straightforward way to read the Tarot. Need some quick advice? An extra perspective on a situation? *Pick a card.* Many people make a daily practice of the one-card draw, to set an intention for the day, to prepare themselves for a specific event, or as a ritual of spiritual affirmation. It begins by thinking of an open-ended question that relates to something in your life that needs more clarity. It can be something as general as "What does today have in store?" to something as specific as "How will I find the patience I need to finish this project?" Shuffle the cards as many times as you need, letting your question crystallize in the forefront of your mind.

Next, you can spread out the cards facedown and let your intuition guide you to one, or simply cut the deck and draw the top card. Any other method will work just as well. Once you have chosen a card, turn it faceup and note if it is right side up or reversed.

Now that your card is revealed, consider its meaning and how it relates to the question you've brought to the reading. *What connections come to mind? How do the characters, objects, or situations in the card relate to your question?* Revisit the card's keywords and description in this guidebook, if you like, and seek out other resources for an even-deeper interpretation.

THREE-CARD SPREAD
WALK THROUGH THE MAIN STAGES.

The three-card spread is a classic spread for Tarot practitioners of any level. This spread takes a wider view at the heart of a question, addressing what has led to it, how it is felt, what stands in the way, what choices remain, and so on. There are several ways to interpret the trio of cards read from left to right, *Past–Present–Future* and *Situation–Action–Outcome* being two of the most popular. These two ways will be covered here, but it will be up to you to decide which makes sense for your practice. As is customary in Tarot readings, begin by thinking of an open-ended question that relates to something in your life that needs more clarity. Shuffle the cards as many times as you need, letting your question crystallize in the forefront of your mind.

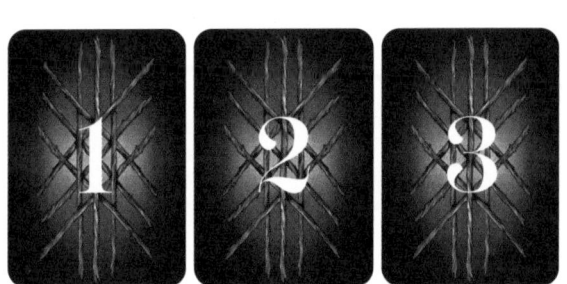

Next, you can spread out the cards facedown and let your intuition guide you to three cards, or simply cut the deck and draw the top three cards. Other methods are just as welcome. Once you have chosen three cards, turn them faceup in an even line from left to right. Note whether each card is right side up or reversed.

The card on the left represents the *Past*, or the *Situation*, depending on what interpretive style you chose. Ask: *What does this card reveal about my past?* or *What events led me to this current issue?* This card is tasked with looking deeper into the choices and consequences related to your question that have shaped your experience.

The card in the center represents the *Present*, or *Action*. Ask: *What do I need to consider about my current state?* or *What actions must take place for change to occur?* This card is tasked with revealing deeper truths about the current moment.

The card on the right represents the *Future*, or *Outcome*. Ask: *What will be different that I cannot understand now?* or *What will the consequences of my actions teach me?* This card is tasked with providing foresight into what may come in the wake of change.

Finally, as you look at the three cards as a set, or a triptych, see if you notice any connections among the suits, the characters, the symbols, etc. Are there any recurring images or objects? Can you picture any relationships between the characters in the cards? Do the meanings of the cards relate to each other or contrast? Is there a story across them? Where is your story in them? Revisit each card's keywords and description in this guidebook, if you like, and seek out other resources for an even-deeper interpretation.

THE CELTIC CROSS
TAROT'S ICONIC AND IMMERSIVE EXPERIENCE.

The Celtic Cross spread is an advanced and exploratory journey through the finer details. If the three-card spread was a step up from the one-card draw, the Celtic Cross is a great leap into the mysteries and complexities of life. It begins with the three Past–Present–Future stages and moves beyond into the metaphysical. As is customary in Tarot readings, begin by thinking of an open-ended question that relates to something in your life that needs more clarity. Shuffle the cards as many times as you need, letting your question crystallize in the forefront of your mind. When you are ready, cut the deck and begin drawing cards. Using the layout pictured, lay each card face-up in order and orientation as shown, until all ten cards are revealed. Begin with the card in spot 1.

Card 1—*The Situation.* This card reveals deeper truths about the current moment you are in.

Card 2—*The Challenge.* This card reveals an issue that needs your attention. It is laid sideways over the *Situation* card, traditionally read as being in opposition, but the two may also work together.

Card 3—*The Root of the Issue.* This card asks you to consider what past experiences, values, trauma, or history are influencing the present.

Card 4—*The Recent Past.* This card asks what recent events have had an impact on your experience or exacerbated an issue.

Card 5—*Possibilities.* This card provides foresight into what may come.

Card 6—*The Near Future.* This card reveals actions and changes that may happen next.

Card 7—*The Self.* This card asks how you yourself have contributed to the situation.

Card 8—*Others.* This card reveals the influence of one or multiple people on the situation.

Card 9—*Hopes and Fears.* This card considers the valuable impact of fantasy and attitude.

Card 10—*The Outcome.* This card reveals the potential endpoint of the previous influences. Not to be considered a reliable prediction, rather, this card points in a direction of where things seem to be going, on the basis of the collective interpretation of the other nine cards. It is a flexible and malleable outcome, though. All the cards in the Celtic Cross are meant to teach us how to aid in what we want for ourselves or to change something we wish was different. Each reading will be different, each bringing new insights and mysteries to find in ourselves.

Finally, see if you notice any connections among the suits, the characters, and the symbols. Are there any recurring themes or motifs? Can you imagine relationships between the people and places in the cards? Do the meanings of cards contradict each other or intensify? Is there a story across them? Where is your story in them? Revisit each card's keywords and description in this guidebook, if you like, and seek out other resources for an even-deeper interpretation.

Thank you for your interest in this Tarot deck, and I hope it brings you insight and empowers you for the journey ahead. The Tarot came to me at a time when I needed it most, and creating this deck was my way of showing gratitude for how it had helped me out of a personal darkness, out of a long night of the soul. I hope to pay forward that help and guidance to you through the imagery and symbolism within these cards.

AUTHOR'S NOTE

There are many traditions and superstitions in Tarot that you have likely heard. What have amounted to a certain set of "rules" on how to acquire a deck, how to store it, how to shuffle it, who can touch it, whom you can read for, how to read reversed cards, and so many more . . . it gets a bit overwhelming. Some say your first deck must be gifted to you; some say you must keep it in a satin cloth. Some say you may never use your deck on yourself; some say no one else may touch it. To me these are rules of confinement, and not of growth. I believe that you do not need rules for reading the cards, and as you familiarize yourself with the Tarot, you may adopt or create any rituals to reading the cards that feel right to you. As the great Tarot master Rachel Pollack says, "Read the Tarot as an act of love." The important part is to feel that you are connected to the process in an authentic way and willing to listen to the insights that may come from consulting the Tarot. Any rules that make you feel phony, or that you will not get the right results if you didn't follow them, are precisely the kind of rules that impede your being open to the possibilities. It's a game of intuition, not strategy. A game that is *inclusive*, not exclusive. And like a game, the Tarot is meant at its core to be enjoyable and challenging, for anyone at any level of experience. I invite you to create some flexible space for how you read and interpret the cards, and with the help of this guide and others, your understanding and depth of experience will grow over time.

On reversed cards: Some Tarot practitioners refer to the alternative "reversed" card meaning when a card is drawn in an upside-down orientation. Some prescribe to the "opposite" approach to the meaning of a reversed card, and some disregard card orientation altogether. This is a flexible decision that you may make for yourself. I've included reversed meanings in this guide because Waite did in his first book on the Tarot, *The Pictorial Key to the Tarot*. Like him, I feel that there is a deeper interpretation to a card when it is revealed reversed, as the descriptions will show.

On the card designs: I had three main goals while creating the *Nightfall Tarot*. First and foremost, I wanted to stay true to the original description and intended meaning of each card developed by Arthur Waite in the Rider-Waite-Smith deck. Second, I wanted to make references to Pamela Colman Smith's iconic compositions, while giving myself some artistic freedom to build upon them, introduce new perspectives, and add more cultural variety. Last, I wanted to make sure that all the images and meanings were linked by the theme of darkness.

On the card back design: The symbol on the back of each card is Skuld's Net, a Norse design more commonly referred to as the Web of Wyrd, the term Wyrd meaning fate. It represents the connectedness between past, present, and future: a net made of nine crossing staves which contain the shapes of all of the Norse runes.

For many people, darkness can be a mysterious and alluring force, a melancholy and protective space, or a place to confront fear. It takes courage to walk through the night, a bit of faith that the road will not end but arrive somewhere in the light. We put one foot in front of the other, we find encouragement in what forms it takes, and we do our best to be there for each other along the way.

I hope that this deck can be a light for you on your journey through the dark.

—AMORY ABBOTT